Every Day Is Mother's Day

Every Day Is
MOTHER'S DAY

Darrin Zeer

Illustrations by Katy Dockrill

CHRONICLE BOOKS

SAN FRANCISCO

Library of Congress Cataloging-in-Publication Data available.
ISBN: 978-0-8118-6084-0

Manufactured in China
Design by Annabelle Gould

10 9 8 7 6 5 4 3 2 1

Chronicle Books LLC
680 Second Street
San Francisco, California 94107

www.chroniclebooks.com

This Book Belongs To

The World's Greatest Mom!!!!!

THANKS FOR BEING SUCH A GREAT

listener, teacher,

cheerleader, doctor, chef,

accountant, therapist, nurse,

comedian, disciplinarian, event planner,

chauffeur, housecleaner,

defender, audience, counselor, tailor,

hairstylist, babysitter,

gardener, dishwasher, teammate,

confidante, arbitrator, entertainer,

chief financial officer, food shopper,

fitness instructor, coach,

interior designer, companion, diaper technician,

and

good friend!

Contents

Quick Help Guide

Introduction

Your life has never been so fast-paced and stressful. It all begins with nine months of pregnancy—including morning sickness, body aches, and mood swings! With love and devotion, you provide years of child care, including cooking, cleaning, diaper-changing, and all the TLC you can muster. You have become an expert multitasker, waiting faithfully on call for your family, seven days a week, twenty-four hours a day. It's a challenge to be the best mom you can be under the pressure and strain of juggling all your family's needs. At the end of a long day of mothering, you may feel mentally drained and physically worn out. You are the perfect example of selfless giving—putting the needs of your family ahead of your own.

This book is meant to provide you, and all hardworking moms, with the rest and relaxation you so deserve. For someone who thinks only of her family, this might seem selfish, but if you take the time to nurture yourself, you will automatically have more energy to give to your loved ones. It may seem like there is not enough time in the day to take care of your own needs, but it can take only a moment. *Every Day Is Mother's Day* offers more than sixty fun and easy ideas to recharge your batteries and provide you with lots of heart, healing, harmony, humor, and happiness. This book will help you take better care of yourself, have more fun with your kids, create more sweet and intimate time with your spouse, and make parenting an easier job. Feel free to simply flip through this book for inspiration; if you have a specific need, look to the Quick Help Guide on page 7.

Happy Mother's Day…
Every Day!

This book is dedicated to you, with love and appreciation!

PART ONE

Heartfelt *MOMents*

Mother's
Morning Meditation

Start your morning feeling peace and love. Set the alarm early to welcome the day; sacrificing a little sleep may help you feel even more rested! Before you get out of bed, spend ten minutes simply relaxing.

- Sit up and get comfortable.
- Take a few deep, gentle breaths.
- Relax your body and mind.
- Focus on everything you are grateful for in your life.
- What amazing things have your kids accomplished? What adventures will unfold today?
- Acknowledge yourself for the beautiful family you have helped create.
- Take pride in what you are doing!

All that I am, or ever hope to be,
I owe to my mother.
—ABRAHAM LINCOLN

Divine Secrets
of the Mama Sisterhood

Are you feeling cooped up and isolated in the house? Or maybe the working-mom grind is wearing you down? Does it feel like no one understands what you're going through? Stay connected by having a phone date with a good friend. Give each other five minutes to talk your worries away. Try not to fix each other's problems; simply listen with lots of care and attention. Listening is a powerful way to support one another. Notice how refreshed you feel once you both lighten your loads. If you are both moms, you probably will keep repeating to each other, "Yes, I know exactly how you feel!" It's important to set a time limit so you can keep things positive—take some time to vent your feelings and then let them go.

Another way to stay connected to other moms is via the Internet. Whatever your concerns, simply do an online search for the answers; you will realize you definitely are not alone. No doubt a mom has written about the subject in her blog, or women from all over have weighed in on the topic in a discussion group. Online social networks are an intimate way to access information and feel connected wherever you are in the world.

> *The best way to cheer yourself up*
> *is to cheer everybody else up.*
> —MARK TWAIN

Housewife Heaven

Sanctuary, serenity, peace, and spirituality are always close at hand. While you're running errands from the mall to the supermarket, to the sporting goods store, and then to the gas station, put spiritual refueling on your to-do list. Step into a church, synagogue, mosque, or park and spend some quiet time. Turn off your phone and embark on a mini-retreat.

- Find a place to sit quietly, and center yourself with a few calm breaths.
- Close your eyes and let your body relax.
- Allow the sacred space to envelop you in calm.
- Remind yourself of the pleasure and honor of being a mom. What are you grateful for? Remember what is important in your life!
- Notice how thoughts of love and gratitude naturally arise after your mini-retreat.

I love you, mom, because…
you always have stood by my side!
—DOUGLAS, AGE 42

Cucumber Pampering

Are your eyes puffy and tired and your feet sore? Try this special spa combo. The cucumber in this footbath and eye treatment will help rejuvenate tired skin and will refresh you in the afternoon before the kids get back from school.

- Slice two to four cucumbers while you're making dinner the night before, and store the slices in the fridge so they'll be nicely chilled.
- Find a basin large enough for your feet and fill it with cool water.
- Keep two to four cucumber slices for your face and throw the rest into the foot basin.
- Place the basin on a towel by your feet; keep another towel handy.
- Place your feet in the basin, and lie back in your comfortable chair.
- Tilt your head back and place one cucumber slice over each closed eye.
- Relax and enjoy your treatment.

I love you, mom, because…
you always make me smile when I am feeling down!
—Rebecca, age 17

I love you, mom, because...
you love me!
—Daisy, age 28

Zen Mom,
Buddha Baby!

See the world through the eyes of a newborn! With memories of your peacefully sleeping infant as inspiration, take a moment to be perfectly still, with no worries about the future or regrets about the past.

Stop what you're doing and sit quietly. For five minutes, do nothing but focus on your breathing. Take a long, deep breath, and imagine you are breathing all the way down to your tip-toes. On the exhale, feel your whole body relaxing, letting all tensions and tightness fall away. Each time you get caught in busy thoughts, simply refocus on your breathing. It takes practice to quiet the mind, so don't stress out about it. Have a pad and pen by your side and write down any important items that come to mind so you can forget about them. Keep returning to your deep, relaxing breaths.

When the five minutes are complete, return to your day, but don't return to the rush. Go slowly and you will experience feelings of contentment and connectedness to your children. Let the magic unfold!

Give Yourself a Hand

You know that being a mom means juggling many tasks at once—all that juggling is literally a vigorous workout for your hands. Normal fluid buildup can occur during pregnancy and may cause mild swelling of your hands and wrists, especially if you're not getting enough rest or drinking enough water. And after pregnancy, Mom's overworked hands need care and attention. Massaging is both very relaxing and medicinal.

Keep a tube of moisturizer in your car's glove compartment or your purse—so it's handy while you're waiting to pick up the kids or are out on errands. Spread moisturizer onto your hands, interlace your fingers, and, using your thumb, massage the palm of your other hand.

For deeper treatment, search out sore spots and then press with your thumb; hold for five seconds. Once you've found all the sore spots, switch hands. Remember to breathe and relax while you massage. To complete, interlace your fingers and squeeze and massage both hands at once, massaging all the lotion into your skin so your hands aren't slippery when you start driving. Notice how good your hands feel and how quickly your tension releases!

A mother is she who can take the place of all others but whose place no one else can take.
—Cardinal Mermillod

Family Circle

Schedule a family night. Plan to spend at least an hour together or, if possible, an entire evening. At the beginning of your time together, you can discuss chores and other family logistics, but try not to focus on that. Once you've quickly taken care of business, move on to having fun and relaxing together.

Massage Exchange This is a great relaxation activity for your whole family. Gather everyone into a circle and have each person turn to their left, so all are facing the back of the family member next to them. Have all family members place their hands on the shoulders of the person in front of them. Squeeze the neck and shoulder muscles of your neighbor slowly and firmly. Show the smaller kids how to lightly pummel the back with their fists. Tell everyone to breathe and let their shoulders drop. If you hit a tight spot, squeeze firmly and hold. Have everyone turn around and repeat this massage technique on their other neighbor. Tell each person something you appreciate about them.

Jam Session Get out your pots and pans, wooden spoons, and anything else that resembles a musical instrument. Appoint a leader to start a rhythm. Follow the leader's beat and see if everyone can play in time with one other. Feel free to sing along and spontaneously hum or whistle. Focus on flowing together in one unified beat. Remember, this is meant to be fun, so don't worry about musicianship!

> *Be kind, for everyone you meet*
> *is fighting a hard battle.*
> —PLATO

Fond Memories

You probably have a baby book stashed away somewhere, but there are just as many special milestones now that your kids are older. Use a beautiful desk calendar to keep track of all your special family moments. Jot down your kids' accomplishments, funny sayings, or any great times you enjoyed together in the daily boxes of your calendar—just a few words can be enough to remind you. When your kids get older, both they and their kids will enjoy your many tales.

If you enjoy writing, buy a beautiful journal and dedicate it to your family. Try this practice at the end of each day before bed: Step out of work mode and into a more relaxed, self-reflective state. Set an egg timer for five minutes and write down important milestones that your children accomplished. During this reflective time, you will get to see just how wonderful and amazing you and your family truly are. *Don't let the miracles of each day pass by unnoticed!*

I love you, mom, because …
you are always there
for me when I need you!
—PAUL, AGE 14

Romance
with a Twist

Yoga is a fun and relaxing way to reconnect with your partner
after a long day of work and parenting. Practice these poses in
silence or while chatting, and enjoy plenty of laughter as you
attempt these moves.

Sorrow shared is halved, and joy shared is doubled.
—Native American saying

Standing Table for Two

- Face each other, standing about two feet apart.
- Grasp your partner's arms, just above the elbows.
- Bend forward with arms interlaced, while taking little steps backward.
- Allow your shoulders to relax and chest to open.
- Breathe together, and relax into the support of your partner for ten breaths.
- When ready, slowly step forward and rise up together.

Sitting Seesaw Together

- Sit on the ground, facing your partner.
- Stretch out your legs so that the soles of your feet touch your partner's.
- Reach out and interlace hands with your partner.
- Take turns stretching forward and back, slowly, in unison.
- Inhale and exhale, supporting each other as you stretch.
- Take ten relaxing breaths, and let your bodies melt into the stretches.

Don't forget to give your partner a wink and a smile!

PART TWO

Healing
MOMents

Work It, Momma!

It really is "survival of the fittest," because without exercise you won't have the energy to get through your day.

Whenever you feel drained, head to the gym for a workout, to do yoga, or to take an exercise class. Working out can be blissful and a much-needed break from the demands of parenting. If you miraculously find the time to add exercise to your schedule, join a gym that offers child care for members. You can also schedule a workout while your kids are on a playdate or at school. This is your private time to push yourself and feel motivated. Coach yourself compassionately, as if you had a kind, internal personal trainer. Repeat a mantra such as, "I'm gettin' my old body back." Savor your great workout buzz by stretching afterward and taking a steam or sauna. Use this positive boost to help you become the best mom possible. If your kids are old enough, try to include them in your exercise routines. Go for a walk in nature or follow a yoga DVD in the living room. Kids love to do yoga! *Fit body, fit mind, happy life!*

I love you, mom, because . . .
you're my inspiration!
—EMILY, AGE 78

Mom's
Belly Massage

Is it any wonder that a mother's energy center is her belly? After all, that's where motherhood starts. In Japan, the abdominal area is referred to as the *hara* and is considered the body's energy center. Stomach massage provides excellent relief for indigestion, tension, and menstrual cramps.

To give yourself a belly massage:

- Lie down and make yourself comfortable.
- Place the palm of your hand over your navel.
- Make gentle circles around your navel in a clockwise motion.
- Try pressing with your fingertips as you continue to slowly circle.
- If you find a tight spot, stop and hold the pressure for a moment.
- Take deep breaths and keep letting your body relax.
- If you are pregnant, avoid pressure on your belly and use a gentle touch. Breathe in and out and feel your hand rise and fall; focus on connecting with your baby.
- If your kids are older, see if they can rub their bellies and pat their heads at the same time. In fact, you should try it, too!

*I am a part of all that I have touched
and all that has touched me.*
—Thomas Wolfe

Mom's
Lower-Back Relief

Between carrying the kids, hauling the groceries, working at your computer, and bending every which way to tidy your home, your body can get sore. For quick and effective relief, try these gentle back supports.

A baby's an inestimable blessing and bother.
—Mark Twain

Legs-Up Stretch

This pose takes the pressure off of the lower back.

- Lie on your back, and slide your legs vertically up against a wall.
- Make sure you are lying back completely.
- Rest your hands on your belly, and close your eyes.
- Feel your lower back loosen.
- Breathe, and forget about your hurries and worries.

Butterfly Stretch

This pose opens the hips and groin region and helps ease backache.

- Lie on your back, with legs bent.
- Bring the soles of your feet together, keeping your feet on the ground.
- Slowly lower your knees outward and toward the ground.
- Place a pillow under each knee if you'd like to ease up on the stretch.
- Simply breathe, relax, and enjoy!

I love you, mom, because . . .
you rejoice in everything I do!
—Daniel, age 63

Pumpkin Smoothie

Pumpkin may remind you of the holidays, but it's actually a great energy booster that you can use all year round! It's packed with vitamin C, which will help your skin stay smooth and help your family fight colds. Share some of this orange drink with your kids and tell them it's a way to celebrate Halloween anytime.

Ingredients

½ cup canned pumpkin
½ cup milk, soy milk, or vanilla yogurt
4 ice cubes
2 teaspoons brown sugar
Dash of cinnamon and nutmeg

Combine all ingredients in a blender and blend until smooth. Pour smoothie into two or three cups. For a fun final touch, add a bit of cinnamon or a few colored sprinkles on top.

Breathing Break

These anytime, anywhere breathing exercises are great escapes. If you find yourself feeling grouchy or stressed, simply sit and put your day on hold wherever you are. You can even try these at work, while sitting in front of a computer screen or with your phone headset on, and no one will be able to tell that you're taking a time-out.

Patient Parent Breath Inhale deeply and slowly, counting as you breathe in. Count as you exhale, and make the out-breath twice as long as the in-breath was. Don't worry about how high you count, just focus on relaxing your entire body and making your exhale longer.

Peaceful Parent Breath Using your right thumb, cover your right nostril and inhale through your left nostril. Place your index finger over the left nostril and pause for a moment. Release your thumb and exhale through your right nostril; pause. Inhale right, exhale left; inhale left, exhale right; inhale right and so on. Slowly repeat for eight to ten breaths and let the peace unfold naturally.

I love you, mom, because … you are my best friend!
—STEPHANIE, AGE 23

Childproof Your Clutter

If you have kids, you have stuff—it's a law of the universe. What's surprising is that, even when you're dead tired, if you take a few moments to clean, you'll actually feel revitalized. Try and take baby steps when putting your home back in order, to avoid getting discouraged. Pick one problem area of the house, such as the front door or the kitchen, and focus your energy there. You're guaranteed more energy, enthusiasm, and peace of mind in exchange for just a few minutes of clutter-clearing. To stop messes before they start, set up a designated space for each of your kids to park their coats, backpacks, toys, and homework. After all, how can they tidy up if there's nowhere to put things?

Pay attention when you're tidying the house—what kinds of clutter do you find again and again? Each week, try to find a home for one piece of clutter. It might mean hanging some hooks or putting up a shelf, but it's worth it so as not to be tripping over the bath toys or slipping on a skateboard. Place an attractive lidded storage bin in the heavy-clutter zones and simply throw everything into the bin. Soon your kids and partner will learn that if they're looking for something, it's probably in the mess bin!

I love you, mom, because...
of your patience!
—LESLIE, AGE 21

A Walk
on the Child Side

This is a fun game for your kids, with relaxing benefits for you.
Lie facedown on the carpet or a futon. Place a pillow or folded
blanket under your ankles and spread a towel under your face.
Have your child stand by your feet, facing away from you. Ask
her to walk on your feet using her heels (shoes off). Have her
walk up and down, applying pressure on different parts of your
feet. Ask her to stop and hold if her heels hit a good spot.

Your child can also experiment walking on other parts of
your body. Depending on her weight, have her walk up your
legs and onto your back. Instruct her to walk on muscles rather
than bones and to avoid walking on the backs of your knees;
make sure it feels good for you. Encourage your child to imagine she is walking on an island, trying not to fall off the island
and into the water—encourage her to move slowly and keep her
balance. Let your child know how the pressure feels. Breathe
and enjoy the wonderful masage.

If you are alone, sit down and place a rolling pin on the
floor under your feet. Roll the sole of each foot firmly over the
rolling pin. Enjoy the soothing pressure!

> *How beautifully everything is arranged by nature;*
> *as soon as a child enters the world,*
> *it finds a mother ready to take care of it.*
> —Jules Michelet

Family Acknowledgments

Part of motherhood is being a disciplinarian, but no one wants to feel like a villain all the time. Create a new family tradition to express gratitude and love and to let everyone know what makes them special: take time over dinner to acknowledge one other with a compliment. Both young and old will be deeply touched by this practice.

To get in the proper mood, have everyone close their eyes, say a little prayer, take a few deep breaths, and let out a big sigh all together. Don't be shy! Then, give compliments such as, "I love the meal you made," "Great job cleaning your room," or "Thanks for being so patient when we went to the store today." The challenge is to make sure everyone keeps their focus on the person receiving, without any side-talking or smart remarks. Watch faces light up as acknowledgments are received!

"Heeling"
Spouse Massage

If you love back massages but just feel too lazy to give them, this technique will hit the spot without anyone having to lift a finger! You'll be amazed at how simple and fabulous the world's easiest massage technique is. First decide who should receive. Have the person who will be receiving sit on the ground, stretching into a forward bend. The giver sits about three feet behind the receiver, lies down, and rests her feet on the receiver's upper back. The giver then presses with her heels, moving them up and down the receiver's back and digging them into the tight muscles between the receiver's spine and shoulder blades. Make sure you both take long, deep breaths together. The giver should ask the receiver how the pressure feels and which area feels best. When the receiver feels completely satisfied, switch places. After you practice this heavenly massage, your backs will feel relaxed, and you will feel intimately connected to each other.

Cleopatra's
Serenity Soak

Throw an extra quart of milk in your supermarket cart and treat yourself to an extra-special spa evening! It is known that Cleopatra loved to luxuriate in a warm milk bath. The lactic acid in milk softens and soothes, and promotes velvety skin. Sure, it's decadent, but you're a queen.

- Run warm water into the bathtub.
- Add a quart of milk to the running water (*a pound of powdered milk also works*).
- Create a Cleopatra-like atmosphere by dimming the lights, lighting some candles, and playing some exotic music.
- Have lots of drinking water close by and a bath pillow handy.
- Sprinkle rose petals in the water for an extra-luxurious effect.
- Soak your worries away and feel like royalty!

*The heart of a mother is a deep abyss,
at the bottom of which you will always
discover forgiveness.*
—Honore de Balzac

PART THREE

Harmonious *MOMents*

I love you, mom, because…
you're the most beautiful woman
in the world!
—Angela, age 6

Mantras for Moms

If you feel tired and cranky and the kids are getting on your nerves, it's time to give yourself a positive pep talk. Listen to the nagging thoughts that plague you, then think up something to balance them. Attach a reminder of your special mantra to the bathroom mirror, the sun visor of your car, the side of your computer monitor, or wherever you'll see it often. Practice mantras to get yourself into the right parental state of mind.

Make up a motivational phrase that is appropriate for you, or try repeating one of these:

"I am proud of myself and my family!"

"I am a good mom!"

"I always try my best!"

"I love my life!"

Mom's
Herbal-Tea Steam

Try an at-home ministeam to refresh your face. Relax and stimulate your senses—using ingredients you probably already have in your kitchen: Peppermint tea is a great natural decongestant and invigorating for the mind. Chamomile is a relaxant, and ginger refreshes the senses.

- Brew a hot cup of herbal tea, using one or two tea bags.
- Slowly lower your face over the cup and inhale deeply.
- Close your eyes for a moment and enjoy the pleasant scent.
- Feel the heat penetrating the pores of your skin.
- Relax and enjoy your moment of peace.
- Don't forget to take a sip!
- Take time to calm and remember the beauty of your life.
- You can use the cold, squeezed-out tea bags afterward as compresses to reduce puffiness around your eyes.

*I think my life began with waking up
and loving my mother's face.*
—George Eliot

Child's Pose
for Parents

This is a wonderful, restorative yoga stretch to try when you need a rest after a long, busy day. Sit back on your calves, lean forward, and rest your upper body on your legs.

- Let your arms rest by your sides.
- Turn your face to one side, or rest your forehead flat on the ground. It's handy to have a towel to rest your head on.
- Let your body relax, and breathe deeply.
- Lie motionless and feel your tension unwind.
- If your child is close by, she may try to climb onto your back.
- See if she can copy you and do the Child's Pose on your back. Both you and your child should just relax, breathe, and enjoy the stretch.
- Repeat this mantra: "I am calm and patient."

Final Doorway Inspection

Whether you have a bunch of kids in tow or are heading out alone, it's important to take pause before leaving the house for the day. Getting everyone fully dressed, fed, and ready to go can be overwhelming. Before you touch that doorknob, avoid unwanted stress by taking a moment to make sure all-important items are packed with you, and that the kids have everything they need.

You can make or purchase a bag with multiple pockets to hang on the doorknob and hold the things you need to take with you when you leave. Family checklists can be helpful as well; hang up a clipboard near the door and post pertinent questions:

"Do we have the keys, watch, wallet, and cash?"

"Do we know how to get where we are going?"

"Do we need to mail any letters or return videos or library books?"

"Do the kids have everything they need?"

"Anyone need to go to the bathroom before we leave?"

Take one last look and a deep breath, and confidently step out the door.

I love you, mom, because . . .
you brought me into this world.
Thanks!
—DENISE, AGE 51

My mother had a great deal of trouble with me, but I think she enjoyed it.
—Mark Twain

Walk It Off

Something troubling you? Kids? Spouse? Finances? Do you expect yourself to be perfect? Do you have mom guilt? Refresh yourself and get some exercise by taking a brisk walk. Put on your walking shoes, bring your favorite music, and head out. With each step, let your expectations go and focus on accepting your motherly abilities.

- ♥ Walk briskly, with your knees up high and posture straight.
- ♥ Feel your troubles melting away with each confident step.
- ♥ Feel the entire sole of each foot as it touches the ground.
- ♥ By the end of the walk, your troubles will have gone.

Temper-Tantrum Training

Whether you're having a disagreement with your child or your spouse, here are some good steps to take when dealing with outbursts. All of us can be susceptible to blowups given the wrong circumstances. Keep these principles in place for the sake of peace:

- Turn your attention to the tantrum thrower.
- Do not try to cut off or calm him down right away.
- Resist the temptation to throw your own tantrum.
- Don't take it personally.
- Breathe, relax, and patiently wait for the release to end.

Most tantrum throwers just need to get it out. If you can remain calm and compassionate, the tantrum thrower will come to his senses and settle down.

The toughest part of motherhood
is the inner worrying and not showing it.
—AUDREY HEPBURN

Happy Housecleaning

Having trouble getting into the right housecleaning state of mind?

- Shake your hands and arms vigorously.
- Shake each leg and foot, one at a time.
- Swing your arms in wide circles—up and around and from side to side.
- Wiggle your whole body till it feels loose.
- Raise your arms above your head.
- Reach your hands toward the sky and rise onto your toes.
- Breathe, stretch, and feel your whole body re-energize.
- If the kids are around, get them involved.
- Try making monkey noises if you really are feeling lazy.
- Turn the tunes up loud and have a let-go dance as you clean.

I love you, mom, because . . .
you think about others before yourself.
You survived breast cancer
and are still living strong.
—JOYCE, AGE 35

How you do anything is how you do everything.
—ZEN SAYING

The Shopping Game

Small children won't melt down in the market if you turn shopping into a game, and older kids will appreciate that the whole thing will take less time if they pitch in. Play the Treasure Hunt game with them. Tell your kids which items you need them to find (for example, laundry detergent and apples). You can even make a simple list for youngsters just learning to read. You may find that your kids are able to shop faster than you. Just relax, and methodically move up and down the aisles while the kids buzz around you. By the time you have covered your entire shopping list, both you and your family will feel the thrill of accomplishment. As you wait in line to pay, present a small gift to your kids as a thank-you for their hard work, such as fruit leather or another healthy snack. They won't drive you crazy with requests for candy if you're ahead of their game!

Hug Your Hubby

It may be better to give than to receive, but the beauty of hugging is that you can give and receive at the same time! Show your husband some affection and appreciation with one of these partner yoga poses. You will be feeling the love in a jiffy, and magically, your stress and tension will vanish.

Happy Hug

- Stand facing each other, with toes touching, and hug!
- Relax deeply into your partner's embrace.
- Breathe five long, deep breaths in unison.
- Let stress and tension melt away.
- Next, slowly rub your partner's back vigorously with your fingertips.
- Massaging between your partner's spine and shoulder blades feels great.

Lap Hug

This is a nice sitting variation to the above hugging technique.

- Sit, facing each other, with your legs resting on top of your partner's legs.
- Sit nice and snug, and give your partner a big hug.
- Loosely wrap your legs around your partner's body.
- Close your eyes and rest your head against your partner.
- Breathe, and feel the love rekindle with your beloved!

Spa Night

This is the kind of multitasking that moms like to do! When you're ready for bed, prepare a miniwrap for your hardest, working appendages. Apply a generous amount of rich, natural moisturizer to your hands and feet. Pull a pair of cotton gloves or socks over your hands and put a pair of cotton socks on your feet; when you awake, both will be remarkably softer.

Sleep Yoga

If you are having trouble falling asleep, this exercise will help you doze off quickly and peacefully.

- Lie flat on your back in bed, with your arms and legs apart.
- Take long, deep breaths, imagining that you are breathing through your whole body. After inhaling deeply, hold your breath.
- Tighten all the muscles in your body and hold tight for a few moments.
- Exhale and release, imagining that each muscle is limp and relaxed.
- Repeat three times, or until you can feel your body melting into the mattress.
- If your mind gets flooded with forgotten to-dos and other thoughts, it may be helpful to write them down on a pad of paper that you keep next to the bed, so you can empty your mind and feel more at peace.

Without kindness, there can be no true joy.
—Thomas Carlyle

PART FOUR

Humorous *MOMents*

*Every beetle is a gazelle
in the eyes of its mother.*
—MOORISH PROVERB

Mom's
Morning Mask

Breakfast will never be the same! Freshen up in the morning
with a wonderful skin softener—this treatment is great for you
and your new look will give your kids something to laugh about.

Ingredients
2 tablespoons plain yogurt
2 tablespoons uncooked oatmeal
A few drops of honey

In a bowl, mix together the yogurt and oatmeal. Add the honey
and stir until smooth. Gently massage the mixture onto your
face, moving your fingertips in a circular motion and avoiding
the eye area. Leave your mask on for five minutes while prepar-
ing your family's breakfast. Rinse off the mask with warm water
and feel your face pleasantly tingling.

Taking the Plunge!

Start your day off with a splash. Rinsing off with very cold water will energize your muscles and help you feel awake. It refreshes your skin, closing the pores, and contracts blood vessels, helping to increase blood flow throughout your body. Plus, a cold-water rinse makes your hair follicles contract and will make your hair appear thicker and fuller.

The adventure begins...
- Start with a warm shower, and do your usual cleanup routine.
- When you're done, slowly change the temperature to cold.
- When the water gets cold, your natural tendency will be to chicken out and run for your life. Instead, sing!!!! Open your mouth and make a noise.
- Focus on trying to relax into the experience.
- Take a deep breath and loosen your muscles.
- It's hard to believe, but you can get comfortable in the cold water.
- Have a soft, fluffy towel nearby to dry off with, and you'll warm back up in no time.

> *I love you, mom, because . . . you laugh at all my jokes,*
> *even if they aren't funny.*
> —PATRICK, AGE 42

Parent Power Nap!

Not getting the rest that you need? Research shows that when a mom's energy begins to wane, an afternoon nap can be just the cure—and unlike a chocolate fix, it has zero calories. In fact, you won't get the munchies as often if you are rested. Thirty minutes or less is all you need to revive. When your baby is napping, you should sneak a short nap and skip the housework. Seek out a quiet nook, set your alarm so you don't worry about oversleeping, and let yourself drift off. Even five minutes can make a difference. You might just be able to steal a few moments while the kids watch cartoons. Your older kids might want to join the nap if you dim the lights and play some relaxing music. The challenge is for everyone to stay quiet. Guide your nap break by telling other "nappers" to take a few deep breaths all the way down to their toes and visualize their bodies floating weightlessly .

A mother understands what a child does not say.
—Jewish proverb

Playground Workout

The park isn't just for kids! Here are some easy ways for you to work out while your children play.

Monkey-Bar Knee Lift

- Firmly grasp an overhead bar with both hands; tighten your belly.
- Test to see if you can hold your body weight using your arm strength.
- Inhale, and raise your knees up in front of you as high as you can.
- Exhale as you slowly drop your legs back down.
- Repeat five times.
- Challenge yourself by holding your knees up for a count of two.

Swing Crunches

- Sit on a swing with your feet solidly on the ground.
- Firmly hold on to the chains.
- Lean back slightly, tightening your belly.
- Exhale, and bring your knees to your chest.
- Inhale, and let your legs back down.
- Repeat five times, and be careful not to flip over on the swing.

Mother is the name for God in the lips and hearts of little children.
—William Makepeace Thackeray

"Yogi Says"

Get your kids to give you a workout! Play this version of "Simon Says" while doing your yoga stretches. Choose one person to lead you through a series of stretches. The leader demonstrates the yoga postures and everyone else follows. When the leader says "Yogi Says," you follow them exactly. If the leader does not say "Yogi Says," stand motionless. The leader gets to penalize the players who mistakenly move. Take turns being the leader. The leader can choose yoga poses like "Tree," "Eagle," or "Cat," or make up stretches. You will get a great workout plus have lots of laughs!

Diaper-Bag Feng Shui

When venturing out of the house with small children, life is a lot less stressful if you've packed everything you need—and you can find it when you need it! The ancient art of feng shui from China, literally "the art of placement," can guide your efforts to be prepared and organized. The stress relief you will derive from being organized is worth the extra time it takes.

When you have a free moment, create a checklist of everything you might need, so you don't always have to rely on your memory. Think about supplies for diaper changes, as well as snacks, toys, books, pacifiers, and other essentials. Store the checklist in the front pocket of your diaper bag, and when you come home from an outing, refill the bag—this way you'll remember that you've just used the last of the wipes. Don't forget to throw in a little something for yourself, like a travel-size bottle of hand lotion or a square of dark chocolate!

A man loves his sweetheart the most, his wife the best, but his mother the longest.
—IRISH PROVERB

Family Circus

If your kids are still small, this is a fun, team-building exercise. These poses are quite advanced, so having dad or someone else stand nearby for support is a good idea. Grab an exercise mat or a nice, thick rug, and tell your kids it's time for high-flying acrobatics!

Airplane   Lie flat on your back on the floor, knees bent. Ask your child to stand facing your feet. Put your feet on your child's hip bones, and firmly take hold of his hands. Slowly pull his hands and lift him up into the air using your leg strength—it will be challenging the first time. Tell your child to imagine he is flying in the sky. When he is ready, slowly let him down. Make sure his feet are touching the ground and he is balanced before you let him go. This pose is great fun for kids, helping them overcome their fear of heights and providing a sense of adventure.

Flying Saucer   Lie on your back with your knees bent. Have your child stand with his feet on each side of your head, facing away from you. Firmly holding each of his ankles with your hands, place your feet on his midback. Once you feel steady, ask your child to lean his body back. With a firm grip, slowly lift him up with your arm and leg strength. Make sure he is comfortable, but ask him not to move around while in midair.

Soccer Mom's
Taxi Service

Attention all road-warrior moms! Ever feel like a taxi driver, having to rush around doing errands or shuttling the kids to all of their activities? And doesn't football practice always end during rush hour? Put your anxiety on cruise control. The sudden urge to hit the horn is always inviting. Challenge yourself to remain calm amid the hustle and bustle of driving. Imagine that the driver in front of you is a close friend, a beloved aunt, or a favorite teacher. Remember that, over the course of your day, a few moments stuck in gridlock isn't such a big deal.

Staying calm not only lowers your stress level, but it also shows your kids how to master their emotions and be patient. Resist the urge to multitask while you drive. Cell phones and other distractions can be hard to resist on the road, but pull over if you need to tend to your kids or talk on the phone. Remember, your family's safety is most important!

Listen to classical music or recorded books to help you relax. Or, just enjoy some quiet.

*Life is not so short but that there is always
time for courtesy.*
—Ralph Waldo Emerson

Steamroll
Your Partner

Even though "steamrolling" might sound like the thing you want to do to your partner when he forgets to take out the garbage (again), it's really a relaxing treat that takes very little effort on your part and will have him moaning with pleasure.

- Have your spouse lie facedown on the floor or a futon.
- Lower your body over his at a right angle.
- Slowly roll your body over your partner like a steamroller (careful around the knees and neck).
- Repeat from head to toe and back again.
- Stop and lie motionless around his midsection and enjoy a stretch for yourself.
- Go slowly, allowing both of you to feel the deep relaxation.
- Breathe together, and experiment with rolling your body in different directions.
- Check in from time to time, and make sure your weight is not too much for your partner.
- If you're feeling adventurous, request that your partner steamroll you!

There is no instinct like that of the heart.
—LORD BYRON

PART FIVE

Happy MOMents

Motherhood
Support Network

The greatest way to rise above your own challenges is to reach out and offer another mom support. Challenge yourself to help another mom once a week, or find ways to partner with other moms to support one other. Try organizing a carpool, babysitting, or helping another mom cook or clean. Tell your mom friend what a great job she is doing. Remind each other not to be hard on yourselves for missing a soccer game or bringing store-bought cupcakes to school instead of homemade. Don't sweat the small stuff. Your positive attitude will rub off on all the moms that you meet.

It's essential that a mom have time for herself without worrying about parental responsibilities, so create a system within your support network to ensure that you and your mom friends are getting this time. Agree to trade nights of babysitting so that you get a date night with your husband or some time to relax on your own.

I love you, mom, because . . .
I was a really difficult kid and
you loved me just the same.
—PHILLIP, AGE 33

God could not be everywhere,
and therefore he made mothers.
—JEWISH PROVERB

Multitasking for Mom

When you have to take care of your life and the lives of your children, keeping everyone's calendar in your head can weigh your brain down. If you don't have a wall calendar, engagement calendar, or PDA that you like, it's time to get one. If you're not a computer person, don't worry about fancy electronics—the goal is to have a system that you really use. And if you love cats, or the mountains, or bright colors, make sure your calendar reflects your personality. Your day and week will go much more smoothly if you jot all your scheduled activities on the calendar. The key to making the system work is to check the calendar regularly—last thing in the evening before bed or first thing in the morning works well.

Make sure your calendar has room for notes and addresses. Organizing your appointments, streamlining your chores, and taking charge of your time will make room for more fun with your family.

Sunday-Morning
Yoga in Bed

Sunday mornings are a good time to be lazy and stay in bed as long as you can. It may be worth letting the kids eat sugar cereals as a special treat, if it means that they'll stay out of your room an extra half hour. Don't agonize—it's worth it!

- Lie flat on your back in bed; take a few breaths and relax.
- Notice any areas in your body that are sore or tense.
- Gently raise your knees to your chest.
- Wrap your arms around your knees and breathe deeply.
- Let your knees slowly drop to one side.
- Enjoy the stretch in your lower back and hips.
- Take your time in the stretch and focus on breathing deeply.
- Slowly release from the stretch and switch directions.

We are all pencils in the hand of God.
—Mother Teresa

Waiting on One Foot!

Try to master the art of patience, and teach your kids how to be truly Zen! This play-anywhere technique is challenging and fun—no matter how old you are.

The trick of this ancient yoga pose is to find your inner strength by standing on one foot. You may be surprised to find your kids have better balance than you! To begin, cross your right leg over the left shin; check to see if anyone is cheating and resting their right toes on the ground. Put your hands on your waist and feel the sole of your left foot rooted into the floor. Feel your posture lengthen and rise upward. Take five deep breaths while focusing on being patient, and then switch legs.

Being patient is not so hard—it just requires practicing on a daily basis. While standing on one foot you may lose your balance; simply reach over and gently take hold of a family member standing next to you. Give each other a helping hand!

I love you, mom, because . . . I do!
—Elizabeth, age 9

Bye-Bye, Baby Belly!

Here are two exercises to help combat baby belly, even if your baby isn't a baby anymore! The best way to get rid of that pregnancy paunch is to strengthen the innermost layer of your belly and repair the separation in the abdominal muscle that occurs during pregnancy.

Belly Breath

- Sit on the floor in a cross-legged position, with your back supported against a wall.
- Place one hand under your breasts and the other on your navel.
- Inhale slowly, and make your belly expand.
- Exhale slowly, bringing your belly button inward toward your spine.
- Hold for as long as you can.
- Imagine your navel is touching the back of your spine.
- Repeat five to ten times daily.

Super Crunch

- Lie faceup on the floor, with your knees bent and feet flat on the ground.
- Place your fingertips, unclasped, on your head.
- Squeeze your belly while you lift your head off the floor.
- At the same time, lift your bent knees off the floor.
- Try to touch your knees to your elbows.
- Lift hips slightly from the floor.
- Hold for a count of two and then release. Inhale up, exhale down through your nose.
- Do two sets of about ten to twenty reps each time. This will help strengthen abdominal muscles and loosen the tightness in your body.

Bump and Boogie

Putting on the stereo and dancing can recharge your body and mind. The more uninhibited you are, the more recharged you'll feel, so get out of your head and into your body. See how many steps you can remember from your school days. Then drop your old steps and explore different rhythms. Follow your kids' leads and do the funky monkey.

Take deep breaths and stretch while you dance. Feel the freedom, get inspired, and enjoy the connection while dancing with your kids.

There is only one pretty child in the world,
and every mother has it.
—CHINESE PROVERB

Mental First-Aid Kit

Learn these simple pick-me-ups and you'll always have something to perk yourself up when your energy is flagging and the day is long.

Instant Enthusiasm

- Find a comfortable place and sit down with your back straight and shoulders relaxed.
- Exhale ten times through your nose in a deep, rapid motion.
- Tighten your belly with each exhale.
- Take a moment to let your breathing return to normal before you stand up and get back to work.

Instant Energy

- Take a long breath in and hold it for eight counts.
- As you hold your breath, try to relax your body.
- Exhale, and hold your breath out for eight counts.
- Again, make sure you don't tense your muscles.
- Let your facial muscles soften and relax, and drop your shoulders down.

The memory of my mother will always be a blessing to me.
—Thomas A. Edison

Mom's
Massage on the Go!

Carrying the weight of the world on your shoulders? Turn your office, car, or kitchen into a spa any time with these easy massage techniques that you can do for yourself. Don't be surprised if you feel the benefits immediately!

Neck and Shoulders
- Place both of your hands on your shoulders and squeeze the muscles with your fingers, rubbing vigorously in circles.
- Focus on dropping your shoulders and keeping them relaxed.
- Gently rub your neck with your fingertips.
- To end, rub your palms together vigorously and gently rest them over your eyes; feel the soothing heat.

Wrists and Forearms
- Wrap one hand around the opposite forearm.
- Squeeze the muscles with your thumb and fingers.
- Move up and down, from your elbow to fingertips and back again.
- Repeat on your other arm.

I love you, mom, because . . . you listen.
—SAGE, AGE 36

I love you, mom, because . . .
you're the world's best chef!
—TED, AGE 56

Health-Food Friendly!

Maintain healthy eating habits for you and your kids! Get creative with nutritious foods, and your family won't even notice how healthfully you all are eating. Keep healthy snacks stocked up in your car and purse to avoid last-minute, junk-food emergency stops that leave you feeling groggy and your kids bouncing off the walls.

Overhauling your diet in one day is overwhelming and will see you running back to your caffeine- and sugar-laden foods of choice. Instead, see if you can gradually substitute healthier snacks in the place of old favorites. Try unbuttered gourmet popcorn in the place of potato chips. Switch from eating chocolates by the handful to a trail mix of nuts, fruit, and chocolate.

Explore exotic fruits and vegetables. Give yourself permission to spend a little more money at the grocery store if it means you'll be excited to try a new, healthful food. Trading coffee for herbal tea is worth exploring, and sparkling-juice mixes are yummy and better for you than sugar-filled sodas.

Finally, try to sneak in healthful additions where you won't really notice them. Tofu disappears into spaghetti sauce. Grind flaxseeds in the coffee grinder and sprinkle them on your yogurt or cereal for a boost of omega-3s. And best of all, opt for dark chocolate over milk chocolate to enjoy the benefits of antioxidants. All things in moderation!

Sweatpants Syndrome

You are a "Hot Mama"! Don't let a little extra weight or stretch marks get you down. When you're busy taking care of the kids, the tendency is to not pay attention to your hair, clothes, and makeup. Just because you're a mom doesn't mean you stopped being a beautiful woman! Take good care of yourself just like you do your kids. Splurge on a new lipstick once in a while. Trade in that frumpy old sweatshirt for a fitted fleece jacket that flatters your curves. Feeling sexy is a state of mind, although nice lingerie can also help! It's nice to look in the mirror once in a while throughout the day and appreciate both your inner and outer beauty. And remember that taking some time for yourself doesn't take away from your family.

Aromatherapy For Mom

When you feel like you just can't take it anymore, it may be
time for a bath. Clear the kids' toys out of the tub, put your
husband on duty, and take some time for yourself. Follow one
of the essential-oil recipes below, and put some conditioner
in your hair, under a shower cap, for a complete at-home spa
experience. These essential-oil combinations can be combined
with Epsom salts to help soothe sore muscles.

Relaxation Formula
4 drops each of lavender and ylang-ylang into the tub

Invigorating Formula
4 drops each of eucalyptus and peppermint into the tub

If one or more of your tiny tots jumps into the bath with you,
put a couple drops of food coloring into the water to add
adventure to your bath experience. It's safe and easy to do.

A hot bath cures all ills.
—Unknown

A Mother's Courage

As told by Darrin's mom, Carole, age 71, about her mother, Olga:

"My mother and father were true partners, raising their six children through the Depression years up in Canada. We lived on a farm in the wilderness with no power or water. My father worked the field with his horse-drawn equipment and lots of sweat and muscle. We were such a happy lot! We kids didn't know that we were dirt-poor. Love and full tummies is all we needed to be happy. In 1944, when I was nine years old, we lost our dear dad from pneumonia. My mother became the sole provider and caregiver for all six of us children, ranging in age between ten months and sixteen years. She never, ever complained once. Work, work, work... wood had to be chopped for fires to help endure our cold winters, gardens grown to last the whole year, clothes mended and sewn on her old Singer sewing machine, wild fruit picked and canned. Although my mother was small in stature, she was huge in determination and ambition, and with the help of the older kids, we managed to survive. My mother spent every waking minute caring for her family—early morning to late night— always optimistic that somehow we all would be OK. She was unwavering, no matter how bleak things appeared. I am proud to call this strong woman my mother and mentor. I am so grateful to have had her in my life, until her death at the grand age of 95. I always felt a deep sense of love, peace, and acceptance when I was in her company.

"I miss her!"

The most important job in the world... is being a mom!
—Darrin Zeer

Acknowledgments

This book is dedicated to my amazing and incredible mother, Carole.
Thanks, Mom, for all you have taught me. I love you!
A special thanks to my loving partner, Daisy Talleur.
Thanks, as always, to Lisa Campbell, Sarah Malarkey, Cindy Ehmann,
Michele Courage, Alison St. John, Patricia Hart, Cheryl Willis,
Jeff Bubar, and everyone else that chipped in and helped out. *Cheers!*

Biography

Darrin spent seven years traveling and study-
ing yoga and meditation throughout Asia. He
is known as America's "relaxation expert" and
currently works as a seminar leader and con-
sultant. He has appeared on CNN and in *Time*
magazine, the *Wall Street Journal,* and the *New
York Times.* Darrin is the author of *Lovers' Yoga,
Lovers' Massage, Office Yoga, Office Spa, Office
Feng Shui, Everyday Calm, Travel Yoga,* and the *Office Stress Emergency Kit*
(all from Chronicle Books).

**Darrin and Daisy teach Lovers' Yoga & Massage retreats around
the world. Darrin leads Office Yoga trainings at corporations
throughout America.**

For more information visit www.darrinzeer.com.